World Faiths

ISLAM

Jan Thompson

Chrysalis Children's Books

WORLD FAITHS

Buddhism Christianity
Hinduism Islam
Judaism Sikhism

First published in the UK in 2003 by
Chrysalis Children's Books
An imprint of Chrysalis Books Group Plc
The Chrysalis Building, Bramley Road,
London W10 6SP

Paperback edition first published in 2005

Produced by Bender Richardson White, PO Box 266, Uxbridge, UB9 4NX

Editorial Manager: Joyce Bentley   Senior Editor: Sarah Nunn
Project Editor: Lionel Bender   Text Editors: Michael March, Peter Harrison
Designer: Richard Johnson   Art Editor: Ben White
Proofreader: Jennifer Smart   Production: Kim Richardson
Picture Researchers: Joanne O'Brien at Circa Photo Library, and Cathy Stastny
Cover Make-up: Mike Pilley, Radius   Indexer: Peter Harrison
Maps and Diagrams: Stefan Chabluk

Thanks to Joanne O'Brien at ICOREC, Manchester, for planning the structure and content of these books.

ISBN: 1 84138 707 X (hb)
ISBN: 1 84458 390 2 (pb)

British Library Cataloguing in Publication Data for this book is available from the British Library.

Printed in China

10 9 8 7 6 5 4 3 2 1

Picture Acknowledgments
We wish to thank the following individuals and organizations for their help and assistance, and for supplying material in their collections: Circa Photo Library: pages 11, 22, ; (Rebecca Thompson) 1, 4, 9, 10, 19, 26, 34, 52–53 ; (William Holtby) cover, 3, 5 center, 5 bottom, 8, 14, 17, 21, 23, 27, 38, 39, 42; (John Smith) 5 top, 6, 7, 28, 30, 37, 54–55; (Christine Osborne) 13, 20, 24, 25, 45, 48–49, 50–51. Corbis Images: 43; (Charles and Josette Lenars) 32; (Earl and Nazima Kowall) 36; (Tom and Dee Ann McCarthy) 41. Topham Photo Library: (Image Works) 12, 18, 35, 40, 44; (Associated Press) 33; (Picturepoint) 31; (Press Association) 46, 47.

CONTENTS

Abdul's Story

Mohammed Abdullah Ahmad, known as Abdul to his friends, is 15 years old and a Muslim – a follower of the religion Islam. He was born in England, after his parents emigrated from Pakistan in 1970. Abdul has an older brother, who has now left school, and a married sister. His father is a pharmacist and was recently elected as a local councillor. His mother works in a hospital laboratory.

'FOR THE PAST four years, I have attended an Islamic boarding school in South-east London. Before that, I went to a local primary school and attended evening classes at the local mosque (where Muslims worship). There, I learned the basics of Islam, and was taught to read the Qur'an, the sacred Islamic book, which is written in Arabic.

The imam – the leader of my community – recommended to my parents that I should be sent to an independent Islamic college, rather than letting me go to the local secondary comprehensive school. At the college, I spend every day from 8 o'clock in the morning till 12.30 in the afternoon on Islamic religious studies.

From 1.45 to 4.45 pm, I am taught the main National Curriculum subjects, including maths, English, science and information technology.

During the first year at my school, boys are tested to see if they have the ability to memorize the Qur'an. If they do, they embark on a three-year course that will teach them to recite the Qur'an accurately and learn it by heart. A Muslim who can do this is called a hafiz. These boys will qualify to be imams – or prayer-leaders, and be able to teach the Qur'an to others.

Some boys show an ability to understand the interpretation of the Qur'an. They take a five-year course, during which they learn the Arabic language, so that they can translate the Qur'an and interpret its meaning. They also study the books of the Hadith. These record the words and deeds of our Prophet Muhammad. I am nearing the end of this course, which will make me an alim – a scholar in Islamic law. I, too, can be an imam – but perhaps in a mosque where the imam will be required to preach the Friday sermon and give people guidance on the requirements of Islam. The purpose of schools such as these is to make sure that Islamic scholarship passes on from one generation to the next.

After finishing at Islamic college, I will probably attend a sixth-form college to study for A-Levels, before going on to university somewhere in England. I would like to serve the Muslim community as a religious leader one day, as well as serving my local community as a councillor, like my father.'

Muslims worldwide

Abdul is just one of more than 1 000 million people around the world who live their lives following the beliefs and traditions of Islam.

EUROPE
Muslims from all over the Middle East have made homes and businesses in most European countries in the past 30 years. There are large Muslim communities in Britain, France and Germany.

ASIA and the MIDDLE EAST
Several countries in Asia, such as Iran, Turkey, Iraq and Pakistan – where this mosque is located – and most countries in the Middle East have populations that are more than 70 per cent Muslim.

NORTH AFRICA
Morocco, Tunisia, Libya, Egypt, Sudan and other countries in North Africa have a predominantly Muslim population. Islam is a major religion in many East African countries, too. Islam was spread through Africa by Middle-Eastern traders centuries ago.

What Do Muslims Believe?

Muslims believe in the one God, whom they call 'Allah', which is Arabic for 'The God'. They believe that Muhammad was the final Messenger of Allah.

THE MOST IMPORTANT beliefs of Islam are summed up in the Shahadah, the Muslims' declaration of faith. It states, in Arabic, 'There is no god except Allah; Muhammad is the Messenger of Allah.'

There are Five Articles of Faith in Islam: belief in Allah, his angels, his Books, his Messengers and Life after death. Muslims believe that nothing can be compared with God, but that there are other spiritual beings – the angels – that are heavenly servants of God. Everyone has two angels looking over their shoulders, to record their good and their bad deeds. To guide people, God sent his prophets, the most important of whom are the Messengers, who brought God's

word in holy books. When Muslims speak the name of Muhammad, or the name of some other prophet, they say (in Arabic) 'Peace be upon him', as a mark of respect. In English texts, it is sometimes indicated by 'PBUH'. Muslims believe this life is a preparation for the next. Their goal in life is to please God and, after death, to be rewarded in Heaven. They want to avoid displeasing God and being punished in Hell.

Why do Muslims believe in God?

We can never fully know or understand what God is like, Muslims say. God is totally different from us: He is eternal, without beginning and without end; He is all-powerful, all-seeing and all-knowing. For this reason, Muslims never try to depict God, and Islam has no images of God.

So how do Muslims know that God exists? They say he has revealed himself in certain ways. There is evidence in the order of the vast universe, and in the diversity in our world, and in the beauty and intricacy in each living thing. Looking at all this, Muslims see the only rational explanation as the Creator God.

They learn about God from their holy book, the Qur'an, which, they believe, contains God's actual words. The Qur'an includes 99 'beautiful names' for God, such as 'The Creator,' 'The Generous,' and 'The Guide'.

The beauty, intricacy and symmetry of nature are some of the reasons why Muslims believe in the Creator God.

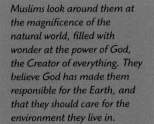

Muslims look around them at the magnificence of the natural world, filled with wonder at the power of God, the Creator of everything. They believe God has made them responsible for the Earth, and that they should care for the environment they live in.

Similarities between Islam, Judaism and Christianity

- All three religions originate from the Middle East.

- They are all monotheistic, believing in one God.

- They share some traditions, going back to Ibrahim (or Abraham).

- Their followers are all 'People of the Book', believing that God's Word is revealed in their holy book.

- All three are ethical religions, concerned to ensure that their followers should lead morally upright lives, in accordance with the will of God.

Muslim students read the Arabic Qur'an so they can learn to recite it by heart. Someone who can recite the whole Qur'an is called a Hafiz.

How did Muhammad receive the Qur'an?

Muhammad was born in about 570 CE (Common Era) in Arabia, in Makkah (often called Mecca), a holy city and a trading centre. He became a trader, travelling across the deserts of the Arabian Peninsula, and coming into contact with Jews and Christians. He was a good man, who became known as 'Al-Amin', meaning 'The Trustworthy'. Muhammad rejected the worship of idols that took place in Makkah, and came to believe in the One God. In a cave above the city, he would spend time alone in prayer.

One night, since named The Night of Power, Muhammad was in his cave when he had a terrifying experience. Muslims say that the angel Jibreel (or

Gabriel) came to him and ordered him to 'read' or 'recite' (the two words are the same in Arabic). Muhammad was illiterate and could not read, but eventually he realized that he must remember the words of the angel and recite them to the people. This happened when he was about 40 years of age, and many other revelations followed. Muhammad passed these on to his followers, who recorded them in a book after his death. This book was the Qur'an, which is Arabic for 'Recitation.' That fateful night changed Muhammad's life and the course of history. He died in 632 CE.

Do Muslims worship Muhammad?

Muhammad always insisted that he was not God, but just a vehicle for God's

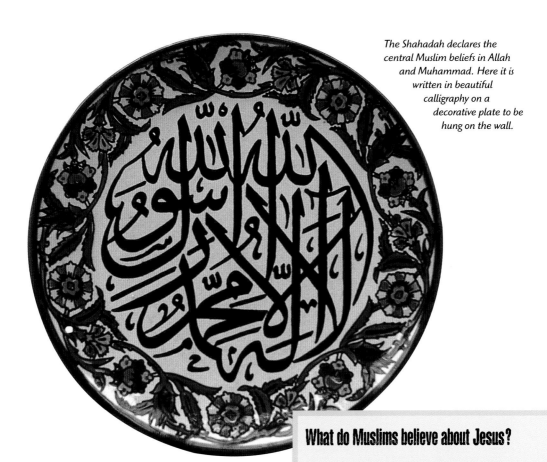

The Shahadah declares the central Muslim beliefs in Allah and Muhammad. Here it is written in beautiful calligraphy on a decorative plate to be hung on the wall.

revelation to the world. He did not want people to worship him after his death in the way that Christians worship Jesus. When he died, his close friend and successor, Abu Bakr, announced his death with these words:
'If there are any among you who worshipped Muhammad, he is dead. But if it is God you worship, He lives forever.'

Muhammad was careful to distinguish between the words he believed were from God, which made up the Qur'an, and his own words. The Qur'an is relatively short, and many Muslims try to learn it by heart. There are also collections of Muhammad's own teachings and deeds, known as Hadith, which means 'Report'.

What do Muslims believe about Jesus?

The Qur'an calls Jesus 'Isa ibn Mariam al Masih' – Arabic for 'Jesus, son of Mary, the Messiah.' Muslims respect Jesus as one of the great prophets, who taught people the Gospel. They believe he was a perfect man, born of the Virgin Mary, who was taken up to Heaven and will return before the Day of Judgement. Unlike Christians, Muslims believe Jesus was a man, not God. Nor do they call him Son of God. Both of these Christian beliefs seem to them to go against their fundamental belief in One God.

What Are The Origins Of Islam?

Historians would say that Muhammad started the religion of Islam in the seventh century. Muslims say that Allah is the founder and that Adam, the very first man, was the first Muslim because he 'surrendered' himself to God.

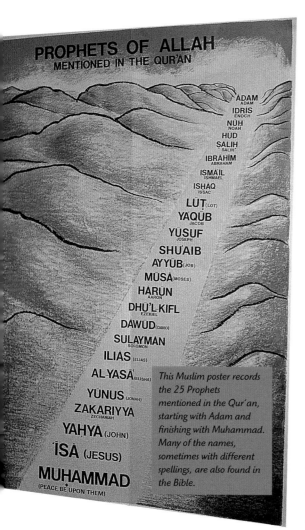

PROPHETS OF ALLAH
MENTIONED IN THE QUR'AN

ADAM
ADAM
IDRIS
ENOCH
NŪH
NOAH
HŪD
SALIH
SALIH'
IBRAHIM
ABRAHAM
ISMĀ'IL
ISHMAEL
ISHAQ
ISSAC
LUṬ (LOT)
YAQŪB
JACOB
YŪSUF
JOSEPH
SHU'AIB
AYYŪB (JOB)
MŪSĀ (MOSES)
HĀRŪN
AARON
DHU'L-KIFL
EZEKIEL
DĀWŪD (DAVID)
SULAYMĀN
SOLOMON
ILIĀS (ELIAS)
AL-YASĀ' (ELISHA)
YŪNUS (JONAH)
ZAKARIYYA
ZECHARIAH
YAHYA (JOHN)
ĪSĀ (JESUS)
MUHAMMAD
(PEACE BE UPON THEM)

This Muslim poster records the 25 Prophets mentioned in the Qur'an, starting with Adam and finishing with Muhammad. Many of the names, sometimes with different spellings, are also found in the Bible.

THE WORD ISLAM means 'surrender' or 'submission'. We all submit ourselves to others. Children are expected to obey their parents and teachers; teachers obey the headteacher or school principal; employees obey their employer and we all have to obey the laws of the land. Muslims believe that God is the highest authority of all, and that he must be obeyed at all times. Obedience to the will of Allah comes before all other obligations. Because Adam worshipped and submitted himself to God, he is recognized as the first Muslim.

The word Islam is also connected with the Arabic word for 'peace'. Muslims believe that obedience to God is the only way for people to find true fulfilment and peace with themselves.

Why are Muslim prophets in the Bible?

A prophet is someone through whom God speaks. Islam recognizes at least 124 000 prophets, because Muslims believe that God has spoken through many people in different ages and different parts of the world. Only 25 of these are named in the Qur'an, most of

Copies of the Qur'an are often decorated with beautiful geometric patterns. The harmony of these intricate designs reflects the order and balance of God's created universe.

The Messengers of God

The most important prophets are the Messengers. They set down the Word of God in holy books. For instance, Moses and the Torah; Jesus and the Gospels; Muhammad and the Qur'an. A passage from the Qur'an reads (in an English paraphrase):

Say: 'We believe in Allah and in what has been revealed to us and revealed to Abraham, Ishmael, Isaac, Jacob, and the Tribes; to Moses and Jesus and the other prophets by their Lord.'

whom are also found in the Christian Bible. Some of their names are slightly different in Arabic. For example, Abraham is called Ibrahim, and Joseph is called Yusuf.

The five major prophets who had lived before Muhammad were, in chronological order: Adam; Nuh (Noah); Ibrahim; Musa (Moses), and Isa (Jesus). Muslims believe that all the prophets were inspired by God and taught the same basic truth, but Muhammad is the 'Seal of the Prophets'. The truth that he brought in the Qur'an, Muslims say, is the final revelation of God for all humankind and for all time. It is the complete and unaltered Word of God, and so there is no need of further prophets after Muhammad.

How did Islam grow?

After his call to prophethood in 610, Muhammad preached in Makkah that there was only one God, the supreme God, Allah. But Makkah was the centre of Arabic religion, where people came to worship idols, and the religious leaders did not take kindly to Muhammad's message. They plotted against him, and in 622 Muhammad left Makkah and settled in Madinah, 480 km away. Here he set up the first Islamic state, run on religious laws. In 630, Muhammad conquered Makkah and established it as the centre of Islam.

Muhammad died two years later in Madinah, by which time he had unified most of Arabia under Islam. This was a remarkable achievement, since many of the Arabian tribes had been feuding with each other for centuries.

In the next ten years, Islam spread beyond Arabia, north-east into Syria and Persia (Iran), and north-west along the Mediterranean coast of Africa, into Egypt and Libya. A hundred years after Muhammad's death, Islam had spread through all the North African countries and into Spain in Europe, and had reached as far eastward as India.

As different dynasties took charge of the Islamic empire, its capital moved from Madinah to Damascus, to Baghdad and finally to Istanbul, where the empire came to an end in 1924. For the whole of this time, Makkah remained the religious centre of Islam, and is so today.

Muslims pray at Juma Masjid mosque in Old Dehli, India, built between 1651 and 1656. Islam reached India in about 750.

A Bedouin about to pray has laid his prayer mat on the sand in the direction of Makkah, the religious centre of Islam.

Who succeeded Muhammad?

The leaders of Islam after Muhammad were called caliphs, meaning 'successors'; and the Islamic empires were known as 'caliphates'. They were not called 'kings' or 'emperors', because they saw themselves as rulers under God, the supreme king. The first four caliphs – Abu Bakr, Umar, Uthman and Ali – between them ruled for over 30 years. They are known as the 'Rightly Guided', and had been close friends of Muhammad from the early days of Islam. Three of them were also relatives: Abu Bakr's daughter, Ayesha, had married Muhammad; Uthman was Muhammad's son-in-law; Ali was a younger cousin and a son-in-law.

The four Rightly Guided Caliphs lived humble lives and were in close touch with the people. But many later rulers were corrupted by wealth and power.

They were no longer elected on the strength of their character, but inherited the position from their fathers. Many became ruthless warriors, bent on conquest.

Muhammad himself had not named his successor. Some people in Madinah thought Ali should have succeeded him. Ali's father was Muhammad's uncle, who had brought him up after his parents and grandfather had died, so Muhammad owed Ali's father a debt of gratitude. Although Ali was younger than Muhammad, there was a close friendship between them. Ali grew up to marry Muhammad's daughter, Fatimah and, after Muhammad's first wife, Khadijah, Ali was Muhammad's first convert to Islam. But Ali did not become caliph for 24 years. His supporters caused a major split in Islam, calling themselves the Shi'a.

Are there denominations in Islam?

Like other religions, Islam has its different branches. About 80 per cent of Muslims are Sunni, whose name means that they claim to follow the right 'path' of Islam. About 20 per cent are Shi'a, which means 'party' because they belong to the party of Ali.

The Shi'a claim that Ali was Muhammad's true heir and successor. They do not recognize the other caliphs, but have their own line of leaders, called Imams, all of whom have been descendants of Muhammad and Ali. The Shi'a are themselves divided into groups, such as the Twelvers, who say that there were 12 Imams, and Seveners, who say that there were only seven. Most Shi'a Muslims belong to the Twelvers, whose main home is Iran, the only Shi'a state.

Among the Sunni Muslims, four main schools of thought have grown up. Among other groups in Islam can be included the Ibadiyyah and the Sufis. Sufism is considered to be the mystical side of Islam. Despite their differences, all Muslims may worship together and may intermarry.

Are all Muslims Arabs?

Islam is the second biggest religion in the world, after Christianity. It has over 1 000 million followers. Although Muhammad was an Arab, most Muslims today are not Arabs. They include Asians and Africans as well as white converts to Islam. But the countries that are almost entirely Muslim are those in the Middle East and North Africa where Islam spread in the early years of its expansion. Much later, in the twentieth century, Islam has spread to other parts of Africa and Indonesia.

The biggest Muslim countries in terms of their land mass are Algeria, Sudan and Saudi Arabia. Each of these is about the size of the whole of Europe. But they are largely desert regions, with low

In 1979, Ayatollah Khomeini's revolution in Iran overthrew the Shah and established the Shari'ah, the Islamic law, as the law of the land. Khomeini and subsequent rulers of Iran have combined the roles of religious and political leaders.

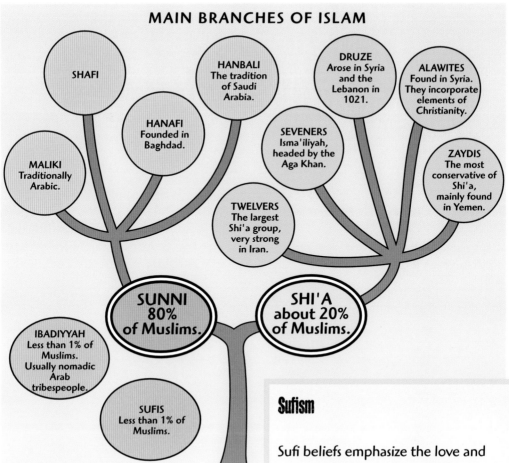

MAIN BRANCHES OF ISLAM

SHAFI

HANBALI
The tradition of Saudi Arabia.

DRUZE
Arose in Syria and the Lebanon in 1021.

ALAWITES
Found in Syria. They incorporate elements of Christianity.

HANAFI
Founded in Baghdad.

SEVENERS
Isma'iliyah, headed by the Aga Khan.

ZAYDIS
The most conservative of Shi'a, mainly found in Yemen.

MALIKI
Traditionally Arabic.

TWELVERS
The largest Shi'a group, very strong in Iran.

SUNNI
80%
of Muslims.

SHI'A
about 20%
of Muslims.

IBADIYYAH
Less than 1% of Muslims. Usually nomadic Arab tribespeople.

SUFIS
Less than 1% of Muslims.

populations. Indonesia, in South Asia, is the country with the highest number of Muslims, about 160 million, followed by Pakistan, with 130 million. India has some 125 million Muslims, although this represents only about 12 per cent of India's huge population, most of whom are Hindus.

Of the traditional Muslim countries, Turkey has been most influenced by the West. Iran became westernized when it was ruled by the Shah, but returned to a very traditional form of Islam after his fall. Saudi Arabia and Pakistan are also very strict Muslim countries, ruled by Shari'ah, or Islamic Law.

Sufism

Sufi beliefs emphasize the love and mercy of God. The Naqshabandi order of Sufis was begun in the fourteenth century and still exists today. It was named after its founder, who wrote these lines (here paraphrased) as part of a prayer:

O my God, how gentle are you with him who has transgressed against you: how near are you to him who seeks you, how tender to him who petitions you, how kindly to him who hopes in you.

What Are The Main Traditions Of Islam?

There are five duties that adult Muslims should follow, known as the Five Pillars. Just as pillars help to hold up a building, so these Five Pillars help Muslims to worship Allah and to lead good lives.

UNLIKE MOST OTHER religions, Islam has no coming-of-age ceremony, when believers promise to keep the rules of their religion. Muslim children gradually learn their beliefs and practices as they grow up in a Muslim home, going to the mosque with their parents and attending the mosque school in the evenings or at weekends. In some Muslim communities, children are expected, once they reach the age of 10, to take on the Five Pillars for themselves. In other communities, puberty is seen as the point at which they become adults and accept these responsibilities.

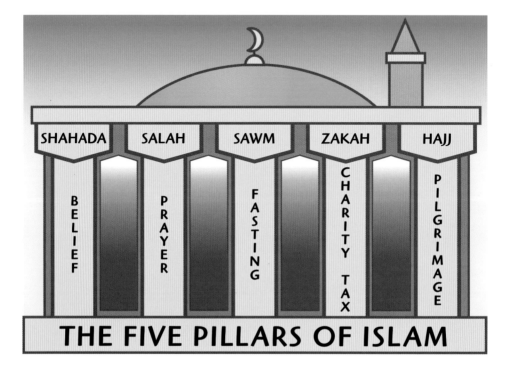

SHAHADA	SALAH	SAWM	ZAKAH	HAJJ
BELIEF	PRAYER	FASTING	CHARITY TAX	PILGRIMAGE

THE FIVE PILLARS OF ISLAM

What are the Five Pillars of Islam?

1 The first pillar is Shahadah – the declaration of belief in Allah as the only God – and belief in Muhammad as the Messenger of God. It affects the whole of a Muslim's life.

2 Salah – ritual prayer – is the second pillar. There are five daily prayers, spread at intervals from first thing in the morning until last thing at night.

3 Fasting, called Sawm, is the third pillar. Muslims fast every year for the whole of the Muslim month called Ramadan.

4 The fourth pillar is Zakah – the charity tax – which is usually paid annually. Muslims are required to give a small portion of their wealth to support the needy.

5 The great pilgrimage – called Hajj – is the fifth pillar. Muslims try to make the pilgrimage to Makkah at least once in their lifetime. But only about 10 per cent of them achieve this, as many are too poor.

Muhammad and the Five Pillars

In 632 CE, Muhammad preached his famous Farewell Speech while on pilgrimage to Makkah. He urged Muslims to keep to their religion. A few months later, Muhammad died and was buried in his home town of Madinah. In his speech, he referred to the Five Pillars:

> O People, listen to me in earnest: worship Allah, say your five daily prayers, fast during Ramadan, give your wealth in Zakah and perform Hajj if you can afford it.

Source: *The Prophet Muhammad's Last Sermon*, translation Al Bukhari

Every day is regulated by prayer, even when Muslims are not in the most convenient place to pray. In Muslim countries, it is not unusual to see Muslims praying out in the streets.

During Ramadan, Muslims go about their daily work and duties almost as normal. In the evening, they will shop for the evening meal that they will eat after sunset. People gather together and enjoy these meals after a long day of fasting.

When do Muslims fast?

Muslims fast during the daylight hours of the month of Ramadan (the ninth month in the Islamic calendar). They must go without food or drink, and abstain from smoking or sex during this time. They should also avoid any bad thoughts, words or deeds.

All Muslims must fast, except for the weak and those who need to keep up their strength. Young children and the elderly would not be expected to fast, nor would sick people, pregnant women, nursing mothers, soldiers or travellers. However, most Muslims fast if they can.

Why do Muslims fast?

The practice of fasting is laid down in the Qur'an. It also says there that Muhammad began to receive the revelations of the Qur'an during Ramadan, making it an especially holy month. When Muslims fast, they are giving up something for God, so fasting is an expression of their faith in God.

Fasting has other purposes too. It allows Muslims to experience hunger, making them more able to sympathize with the poor, who often go hungry. It tests their powers of endurance, so that they will be strong enough to cope with whatever life has in store. It helps them learn self-

Muslim Aid is an international relief and development agency working among poor Muslim communities.

DEBATE - Should you give to charity?

- Yes. We are born into an unfair world, where the three richest people in the world are wealthier than the 48 poorest countries combined, and where 12 million children under five die each year from poverty-related illness. Those of us who have more than we need should help those who lack even their basic needs.

- No. People deserve the money they have earned and should spend it as they wish. Charity demeans people and makes them dependent on others.

Statistical source: World Development Movement

control, making them less selfish and more able to resist evil.

Why do Muslims give to charity?

Islam encourages people to work hard and be generous to others. Muslims must give at least 2.5 per cent of their wealth to those in need. In some Muslim countries this is collected, like income tax. In others, it is left to the individual to decide to support a Muslim charity, such as Muslim Aid. Bangladeshis working abroad send the money home to help the community.

The word Zakah means 'purification'. Giving away a percentage of your wealth, Muslims believe, purifies the rest for your own use. If God blesses your labours with rewards, you should thank God and enjoy your wealth, sharing your blessings with others.

Do Muslims have rites of passage?

Islam has few rites of passage, the most important ones being at birth and death. Most others are cultural rather than religious ceremonies and differ from one country to another. There is no coming-of-age ceremony as such, but in Turkey, boys are circumcised between the ages of 7 and 10, and this is treated as an initiation into manhood.

What happens when a baby is born?

The birth of a new baby is a cause for much celebration in Islam. Every child is a gift and blessing from God.

When the baby is seven days old, the aqiqah ceremony takes place. The baby's hair is shaved off and weighed, and the same weight in gold or silver is given to the poor. Even if the baby is bald, a donation is still made. To give thanks for the child, two sheep or goats are killed for a feast if it is a boy, or one for a girl. The meat is shared with the family and

Fourth birthday

By the age of four, Muslim children are expected to be able to say the Arabic words *Bismillah–ir–Rahman–ir–Rahim*, meaning 'In the name of God, the Merciful, the Compassionate'. This is the opening of almost every chapter of the Qur'an, and the words are frequently spoken by Muslims. Learning to say this marks the beginning of a child's Islamic education, after which he or she will be taught to pray.

The call to prayer is whispered in the baby's ear, beginning with: 'Allah is great. I bear witness that Muhammad is the Messenger of Allah.'

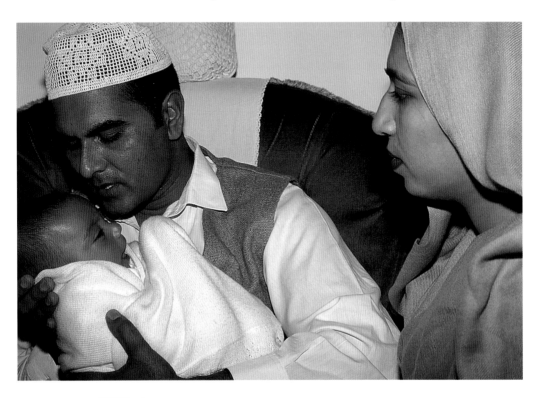

visitors, and a third of it is given to the poor. Often baby boys are circumcised at this ceremony.

The most popular name for a boy is Muhammad, after the Prophet. Many other boys' names start with 'Abd', meaning servant, such as Abdullah ('servant of God') or Abdul Rahman ('servant of the Merciful', another name for God). A girl might be called Ayesha (after one of Muhammad's wives) or Fatimah (his daughter).

What happens when Muslims die?

When a Muslim dies, the body is washed, wrapped in a shroud with the face uncovered, and buried as soon as possible, out of respect for the dead person. Cremation is forbidden in Islam because it is believed that the body will be raised up at the Last Day. The funeral service is simple, and usually attended only by men. Those present at the graveside say a funeral prayer, asking for Allah's forgiveness for the dead person's sins, so that he or she will go to heaven. The body is laid in a grave with the head turned to the right, facing Makkah, the direction of prayer.

Muslims do not encourage mourning or any elaborate ceremonies when someone dies. They have a strong belief in an afterlife and in the mercy of God for believers. It is important to them that they show acceptance of God's will over life and death.

Muslim graves all point the same way, so that the body faces Makkah. This Muslim cemetery is in Rawalpindi, Pakistan. In most Muslim countries, a grave will be no more than a mound of earth marked with a simple headstone.

Do Muslims celebrate their faith?

Compared with other religions, there are relatively few festivals in Islam. The two main ones, which all Muslims celebrate, are Id-ul-Adha ('The Great Festival'), the festival of sacrifice at the end of Hajj; and Id-ul-Fitr ('The Little Festival'), the festival of fast-breaking at the end of Ramadan. Besides these, there are several other important days in the Muslim calendar. In Muslim countries, Id-ul-Fitr is celebrated with a national holiday of up to four days.

At festival time, Muslims send greetings cards decorated with Arabic words from the Qur'an, with beautiful patterns or with pictures of famous mosques. Because Arabic is written from right to left, the cards often open the opposite way to western cards.

Muharram is the first month of the calendar, and the first day of this month is New Year's Day, called Al Hijrah. It commemorates the day known as the 'Hijrah', or emigration, when Muhammad left Makkah to settle in Madinah. Muslim years are counted from this event in 622 CE. The year 2000 CE was the year 1421 AH (after Hijrah) in the Muslim calendar.

Ashura, which falls on the 9th and 10th days of Muharram, is kept by Shi'ite Muslims as a day of fasting and mourning for the death in battle of the Prophet's grandson, Hussein.

The 12th of Rabi al-Awwal is Maulid ul Nabi – the Prophet's birthday. There are processions and people listen to stories about Muhammad's life.

Islamic months and years

Muslim festivals fall on the same date each year in the Muslim calendar, but the 12 months of its year begin with the new moon. This makes its months shorter than those in the western calendar, and its year 10 or 11 days shorter. Thus, Muslim festivals are not seasonal festivals like those of other religions, because they take place about 10 days earlier each year and move back through the seasons.

As part of a festival celebration, Muslims eat samosas at a street stall in Pakistan. The Muslim word for festival is 'Id', meaning 'returning at regular intervals'.

The 27th of Rajab is Lailat-ul-Isra'wal Miraj, commemorating the miraculous Night Journey of Muhammad from Makkah to Jerusalem and his ascension into heaven and return. Extra prayers are said that night.

The night of the 14–15th of Shaban is Lailat-ul-Barat, the Night of Forgiveness when, Muslims believe, God decides what will happen to each person in the coming year. It is a time to repent of your sins and ask God for forgiveness. Many Muslims will stay awake all night, reading the Qur'an.

On the 27th of Ramadan, Lailat-ul-Qadr honours the Night of Power, when Muhammad is said to have received his first revelation of the Qur'an. Many Muslims spend all night at a mosque, reading the Qur'an and praying.

Muslim festivals are religious occasions –
opportunities to praise God, to remember
the poor and to gather together,
encouraging each other in the faith.

How is Id-ul-Fitr celebrated?

Id-ul-Fitr is the day of rejoicing at the
end of Ramadan, when the long month
of fasting is over. It takes place on the 1st
of Shawwal, which is signified by the
sighting of the new moon. In Muslim
countries, there is a national holiday of
up to four days. In western countries,
Muslims take the day off work or school.

Children especially enjoy the festival,
because they receive presents such as
sweets, money and new clothes.
Families clean their homes and decorate
them with greetings cards. They also
invite relatives and friends to their
homes to share their food.

The day begins with a visit to the
mosque. So many families attend that it
is often necessary to have several
morning prayer-sessions or to create
more space by laying down sheets

outside the mosque where people can
pray. Birthdays that fall during the
month of Ramadan are celebrated at
Id-ul-Fitr, and many weddings take
place then, too. Families also remember
their deceased relatives and visit their
graves at this time.

The fast of Ramadan helps Muslims to
sympathize with people who go hungry,
so Id-ul-Fitr is an occasion for sharing
with the poor, and is sometimes called
the Festival of Charity. Every Muslim
who can afford it donates the cost of a
meal. The money is often collected
beforehand so that it can be distributed
in time for the poor to enjoy the festival.

Why do Muslims sacrifice animals?

Many Muslims like to eat meat at festival
times, even if they are too poor to do so
regularly at other times. When Muslims
kill an animal for food, they 'sacrifice' it,

as part of their religion, to remind themselves that they are taking a life and to thank God for his gift of life.

At Id-ul-Adha, Muslim families sacrifice an animal at the same time as pilgrims on the Hajj to Makkah are doing the same. A family might offer a goat or sheep; a larger group could offer a camel or a cow. The festival is a time to eat well with family and friends, but also to remember the poor, who receive a third of the meat.

Id-ul-Adha is the Festival of Sacrifice, when animals are killed for food. Families offer their best animal, to give thanks to God.

Ritual slaughter

The Muslim method of killing an animal is to slit its throat, while saying the Bismillah prayer. Only then is the meat considered to be halal, or 'permitted'. There is much controversy in western countries over the ritual slaughter of animals. Scientists cannot agree on which method of slaughter causes the animal the least pain and trauma. Muslims believe that their method is the least painful way for the animal to die, particularly if it is killed at home, and spared the trauma of a journey to the abattoir.

How Do Muslims Worship?

The whole of a Muslim's life is worship. The five main duties – the Five Pillars – are all ways of worshipping Allah. Muslims pray five times a day, as set down in the Pillar known in Arabic as **salah**.

MUSLIMS LIKE TO say salah (prayers) together with other Muslims, whenever possible. The main act of worship of the week, called *jumu'ah*, takes place shortly after midday on Fridays. This includes a sermon from the imam, who leads the prayers. Muslims also say their own private prayers during salah.

Why do Muslims wash for prayer?

Being clean in the presence of someone important is a mark of respect. Muslims pay God respect by washing before they pray, as God is the most important being in their lives. Washing also has a practical purpose. It is refreshing and helps the person praying to concentrate. Islam came from Arabia, a hot, desert

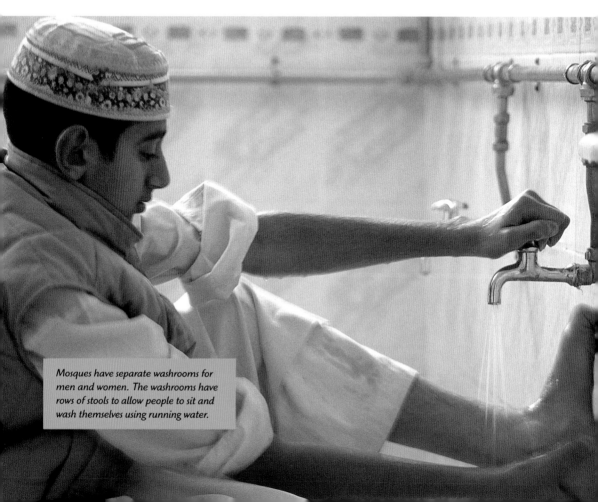

Mosques have separate washrooms for men and women. The washrooms have rows of stools to allow people to sit and wash themselves using running water.

When Muslims pray, they line up together from the front, standing shoulder to shoulder. This is a sign of their unity and equality before God – no one is so important that they should stand apart from the rest.

country; and many Muslims still live in hot countries today. Washing also reminds Muslims of prayer, because they can apologize to God for sins, and wash them away.

How do Muslims wash before prayer?

There is a special way that Muslims wash before prayer. It is called *wudu* in Arabic. First, they wash their hands thoroughly, then their mouths, nostrils and faces, three times. Next, they wash their arms three times. They run wet hands over their head, wiping their neck and their ears. Lastly, they wash their feet thoroughly up to the ankle, starting with the right foot.

Why people pray

Prayer is an important element in all religions. It can take different forms. Prayer can be a way of speaking to God, or of listening to God in silence. People of all ages can find prayer very satisfying. They can use it to ask God for forgiveness when they feel guilty; they use it to praise God and to thank God for all the blessings in their lives; and they can pray for other people as well as for themselves.

Muslims prostrating themselves in prayer before God. Prostration is not the most modest position, which is one reason why men and women pray separately and must dress modestly for prayer.

How do Muslims pray?

There is a series of movements that Muslims make when they pray. It is called a *rak'ah* in Arabic. Different prayer sessions have two, three or four rak'ahs. A rak'ah consists of standing, bowing and two prostrations, while reciting prayers and passages from the Qur'an.

Standing and bowing show respect to God. Prostration shows more because, if you kneel down on the floor with your forehead touching the ground, you are completely helpless. It is a sign of submission. Muslims do this to show that they are entirely at the mercy of God. Prostration is the most important of the prayer positions: it shows what

'Islam' means – 'submission' to Allah. 'Muslims' are people who submit themselves and their whole lives to God.

Muslims finish their prayers by sitting back on their heels and turning their heads to the right and then to the left, saying 'Peace be on you, and Allah's blessings.' This shows their concern for the people next to them, and for all their Muslim brothers and sisters throughout the world.

Where do Muslims worship?

Muslims can worship God anywhere, as long as it is a clean place for them to put their forehead down on the ground in prostration. They often use prayer-mats for this purpose. A place of prostration is called a mosque, or *masjid* in Arabic. We tend to think of mosques as special buildings, with domes and tall towers. But many mosques in hot countries are simply courtyards where Muslims can line up together in prayer. There must be somewhere for them to wash and somewhere to put their shoes. To keep the prayer hall clean, shoes are not allowed inside.

The mosque must have separate areas for men and women, so that they do not distract each other. It needs a marker, such as an alcove or niche in the wall to indicate the direction for prayer (towards Makkah), and it must have a raised platform, called a minbar, for the imam to preach the Friday sermon.

DEBATE - Do religious believers need a special place of worship?

- No. It is not right to spend money on places of worship when people are starving all over the world. Moreover, if God is everywhere, what need is there for special places of worship?
- Yes. Believers should be allowed to give God their very best, whatever it costs. The design of the building can create a setting that helps people to worship.

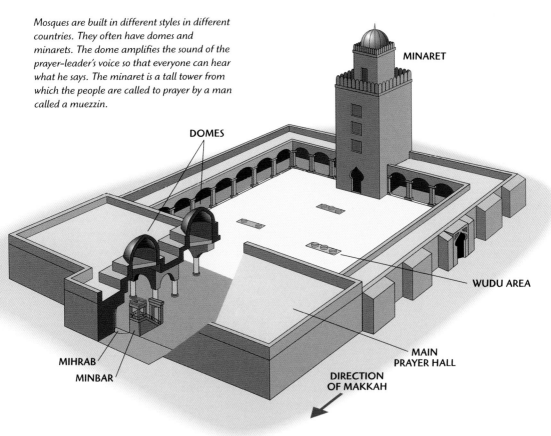

Mosques are built in different styles in different countries. They often have domes and minarets. The dome amplifies the sound of the prayer-leader's voice so that everyone can hear what he says. The minaret is a tall tower from which the people are called to prayer by a man called a muezzin.

MINARET

DOMES

WUDU AREA

MIHRAB

MINBAR

MAIN PRAYER HALL

DIRECTION OF MAKKAH

Why is pilgrimage important to Muslims?

The Hajj, the Great Pilgrimage to Makkah (now in Saudi Arabia), is one of the Five Pillars of Islam. It takes place on the 8–10th of the twelfth month, called Dhu-l-Hijjah.

Pilgrims are proud to walk in the footsteps of Muhammad, who himself made the pilgrimage, and to remember the earlier prophets Ibrahim (Abraham) and his son Isma'il (Ishmael). Makkah is such a holy city for Islam that only Muslims are allowed there, and they have to show their visas at checkpoints around the city. Each year, some two million pilgrims gather in Makkah during the Hajj.

Muslims spend the days of Hajj in regular prayer, reading the Qur'an and performing the rituals of the pilgrimage. It is an opportunity to renew their faith and to ask God to forgive them their sins and transgressions.

Why is the Ka'bah the centre of Islam?

Muslims spend their lives praying in the direction of the Ka'bah, before they ever get the chance to see it – if ever they do. The Ka'bah is the building in the centre of the Sacred Mosque in Makkah, and the pilgrimage starts with the pilgrims circling it seven times continuously in an anticlockwise direction. Muslims believe that it was the first house of prayer on earth, built by Adam, the first man, as a replica of the house of prayer in heaven. Later, the prophet Ibrahim (or Abraham) is said to have rebuilt the Ka'bah with the help of his son, Isma'il.

In one corner is the Black Stone, which pilgrims try to touch or kiss. This was part of the Ka'bah long before the time of Muhammad. There is a story of how once, when the Ka'bah was being repaired, Muhammad was asked to mediate between the chieftains of Makkah, who each wanted the honour of replacing the stone in its wall Muhammad suggested each chief should hold a corner of a cloak on which the stone was carried, and Muhammad lifted it into place.

	90 – 100% Muslim
	50 – 90% Muslim
	25 – 50% Muslim

North Africa and the Middle East are the historical heartlands of the Islamic faith. Saudi Arabia, where all the greatest Islamic shrines are to be found, is the most important country for Muslims in the region.

Pilgrims massed in the courtyard of the Great Mosque, where the Ka'bah stands. The Ka'bah, which takes its name from its cube shape, is covered in a black cloth embroidered with passages from the Qur'an.

Pilgrimage in religion

A pilgrim is someone who makes a special journey, called a pilgrimage, to a holy place. Places become centres of pilgrimage usually because they are associated with important people or events in the history of the religion. A pilgrimage is done as an act of worship. All major religions have their places of pilgrimage, but only Islam makes pilgrimage into a duty that its followers are expected to perform, if they are able.

At that time, the Ka'bah housed many religious idols. When Muhammad later conquered Makkah, he destroyed the idols in the Ka'bah. Today, the building remains completely empty as a sign to Muslims that they must never try to make images of God.

The pilgrimage of life

Life is a journey: from birth to death, and maybe beyond. Many religious people see the journey of life as a pilgrimage: a journey with God, bringing them closer to God. This is why important stages in life are marked by religious rituals, praying for God's guidance and blessing, as they move from one part of their journey to the next.

What is the most important part of Hajj?

The most important event of Hajj takes place on the second day, in the Plain of Arafat, about 24 km outside Makkah. Pilgrims must be there from noon to dusk. Most of them arrive in the morning, on foot or in buses and coaches. They encamp on the desert plain, creating a huge tent city.
In the middle of this plain stands the Mount of Mercy, where pilgrims pray to God for forgiveness of their sins. The spectacle of many thousands of people swarming over this hill, their hands and faces raised to God in prayer, makes Muslims think of the Last Day – the day when, they believe, the world will end and God will judge each individual soul. Praying here at Hajj, on the Mount of Mercy, is intended to gain God's forgiveness and mercy, so that they will go to heaven when they die.

What else happens at Hajj?

On the third day of Hajj, as the pilgrims travel back towards Makkah, they stop at the town of Mina. Here they throw seven small pebbles at each of three stone pillars. This ritual, called 'stoning the Devil', is an expression of their rejection of evil and their determination to withstand temptation.

Later, the pilgrims remove their special clothes, wash themselves and cut their hair to show that they are no longer in ihram. They are now free to relax together and enjoy the festival of Id-ul-Adha. The festival is held at Mina and begins with a big feast. Pilgrims must offer an animal for sacrifice, if they can afford it. If they cannot, they will share in the third of the meat set aside for the poor. As there is too much meat to distribute all at once, the Saudi government has installed refrigeration. The sacrifice of animals reminds Muslims of how Ibrahim was commanded by God to sacrifice his son Isma'il. At the last moment, God substituted a ram for the boy. Three times, the Devil is said to have tempted Ibrahim not to sacrifice his son, and Isma'il to run away. But both father and son were determined to obey God, whatever the cost. It is said that together they drove away the Devil with stones, hence the traditional stoning of the three pillars at Mina.

Many pilgrims go on from Makkah to visit Madinah, where Muhammad lived for the last ten years of his life, and is buried. Some also go on to Jerusalem, the third holy city in Islam.

Muslim pilgrims on the Hajj.

What Are Muslim Values In The Modern World?

Muslim values have not changed since the time of Muhammad and the revelation of the Qur'an. They are based on truthfulness and honest living; responsibility and trustworthiness; kindness and compassion; forgiveness and generosity; humility and modesty; fortitude and courage.

THE MOST IMPORTANT authority in life for Muslims is Allah, whose words, they believe, are recorded in the Qur'an. What God tells Muslims to do there, they should do; and what God forbids, they should not do. Muslims also look to the Prophet Muhammad for guidance, which is called the Sunnah – his practice or way of doing things. In his Farewell Speech, Muhammad said, 'I leave behind me two things, the Qur'an, and my example, the Sunnah, and if you follow these you will never go astray.' Islamic Law is called the Shar'iah, the 'straight path', and is based on the Qur'an and the Sunnah.

Some things, such as the Five Pillars, must be done. Other things, for example adultery, are completely forbidden. In between, are things that are approved of and others that are not – down to actions that are left to the individual's conscience. Many modern issues, including organ transplantation, come into this last category.

What are arranged marriages?

Marriage and family life are at the heart of Muslim society. Early marriage is seen as the best channel for sexual desires, to allow them expression in having children and grandchildren in a secure setting, and to give people companionship with a partner.

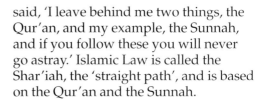

This Muslim boy is looking up a Hadith of the Prophet Muhammad. Each Hadith is a 'statement' of witnesses to what Muhammad said and did.

A Muslim couple getting married in Malaysia. They will have been introduced to each other by their parents, rather than have met each other by chance.

Because of the importance of marriage, it has always been the custom in Islam for marriages to be arranged by the parents. Marriage is seen as joining two families together, rather than just two individuals. A boy's parents will look for a suitable partner for their son, and approach the girl's parents. The boy and girl meet in a family gathering, and both should give their consent. An arranged marriage should not be a forced marriage, which is against Islamic law. In the West, most people marry someone whom they love. In an arranged marriage, it is believed that love will grow in time between the couple.

DEBATE - is arranged marriage a good idea?

- Yes. Our parents have experience and can make a wise choice. They know us and want the best for us. There are fewer divorces. Most of the world's population have arranged marriages.

- No. People should choose their own partners. If the marriage does not work out, the couple should be free to divorce without fear of tearing the family apart. Arranged marriages go against these freedoms.

A Muslim with his two wives and children. It is expensive to keep more than one wife, and these days most Muslims do not practise polygamy.

Can Muslim men have several wives?

Strictly speaking, polygamy – the practice of having more than one wife at a time – is permitted in Islam, although it is not common. The practice goes back to Muhammad's time, when many young men were killed in battle, leaving widows and children in need of support and protection. After his first wife, Khadijah, died, Muhammad had at least nine more wives. The Qur'an states that a man may take up to four wives at a time, provided that he treats all of them equally. Even today, some of the more wealthy Muslims follow this practice in countries where it is permitted.

Why is adultery such a serious offence?

'You shall not commit adultery, for it is foul and indecent."
Source: *The Qur'an 17:32.* Penguin Books 1974

Adultery – having sex, if you are married, with someone other than your husband or wife – is a very grave sin in Islam and is strictly forbidden. Muslims believe that the people involved have acted irresponsibly, giving way to lust and showing no concern for other adults and any children who may be affected by their actions. Adultery threatens a marriage and family life, besides raising the risk of illegitimate children. In strict

Muslim countries, such as Saudi Arabia and Iran, the Shari'ah (Islamic Law) is the law of the land and punishment for adultery can be very severe.

Is divorce allowed?

Islam recognizes that a marriage may not work. It does not condemn a married couple to a life of misery by refusing to consider the possibility that it can be better for a couple to separate and lead new lives. Muslims would prefer to avoid divorce, but it is permitted if it is not possible to save the relationship. It is far better to divorce and remarry than to commit adultery, which is forbidden. Married couples are separated openly and legally, with their rights protected.

Why are the elderly shown respect?

Muslims have traditionally lived in extended families. A new bride will move to her husband's home and live there with his parents and other relatives. In this type of family, people of all ages have to learn to get on together and everyone is looked after, from the little children to the great-grandparents.

The Qur'an on elderly parents

Your Lord has commanded you … to be kind to your parents. If one or both of them reach old age when they are with you, do not speak impatiently to them or scold them, but speak to them respectfully. Act humbly towards them and show kindness and say, 'My Lord, show them mercy, as they cared for me when I was a child.'

English paraphrase of *The Qur'an* 17: 23–24

There is much love for children in Islam, and couples often have large families. Children, in turn, are brought up to respect their elders and to accept the fact that the younger generations will be responsible for looking after the elders as they grow old and frail.

Muslim families prefer to keep their elderly relatives with them at home, rather than put them into care.

Do women have rights in Islam?

Islam teaches that men and women are equal before God, but that he has made them different for different roles and responsibilities in life. Muslims believe that motherhood is a blessing from God and an important part of being a woman, and a woman's first duty is to her family. Women are not thought of as being less important than men. Their influence in bringing up their children is of utmost importance, and mothers are given great respect.

Can Muslim women work?

Many Muslim women are highly educated and have responsible jobs, such as teaching or being a doctor. Some have achieved important public positions, such as Benazir Bhutto who, as Prime Minister of Pakistan in 1988, became the first woman to run a Muslim state. But most Muslim women in a profession would expect to take a break from their careers to look after their children when they are young.

The cultural traditions of some Muslim countries, like Egypt, Morocco and Saudi Arabia, prevent women from doing much outside the home. In other Muslim countries, such as Turkey and Iran, girls as well as boys are educated and may go on to university and a

In some strict Muslim countries, women are required to wear a chador over their other clothes when they appear in public.

Most British schools now make allowances for Muslim girls to cover their heads and legs, and to wear tracksuits for sports.

professional career. In the West, many Muslim girls will have similar career plans to their non-Muslim friends.

What do Muslim women wear?

All Muslims – men and women – are taught to dress modestly. This is laid down in the Qur'an, though it is interpreted differently in different Muslim countries. In public, women are generally expected to wear the hijab, which often consists of just a scarf to cover their hair, rather than a full covering of the face. Many Muslim women feel very comfortable with the Islamic dress code. They believe it protects them from unwanted attention from men, and helps them to be treated equally and with respect.

Islam and sex

Sex is seen as natural and a gift from God – provided that it is not abused. It should be enjoyed by a husband and wife, within a stable marriage. Islam does not encourage celibacy (doing without sex altogether) – there are no monks and nuns in Islam. Islam does encourage young people to marry early, to allow expression of their sexual desires in a stable setting. Boys and girls over ten are not allowed to mix freely together, and Muslim parents keep a close eye on their teenage children, to prevent them from being led astray.

Abuse of drugs and drinking alcohol are forbidden in Islam.

Why is Islam against alcohol?

Alcohol, in the form of beer, wine or spirits, is often consumed in western society, but the Qur'an forbids it. In many western societies, drinking alcohol is associated with special events such as restaurant meals, parties and weddings, but it is also an integral part of everyday social relations for many people. Unfortunately it is also associated with uncontrolled behaviour and with road accidents in which innocent people are killed or injured by drunken drivers. Television campaigns attempt to remind people of the dangers of drinking and driving. Excessive drinking can also cause fatal medical conditions such as cirrhosis of the liver. Some people become addicted to alcohol, and it is difficult for alcoholics to give up drinking in societies where alcohol is easily obtained.

There was similar abuse of alcohol in Muhammad's day; the harm that it caused far outweighing any pleasure that it brought. Islam teaches that people should respect and look after the bodies God has given them. It is important that Muslims are in full possession of their senses when they pray – which they do five times a day, four of these after midday, when people are most inclined to have an alcoholic drink.

Young British Muslims

Sixty per cent of Muslims in the UK are under 25 years old. Most of them were born here and have English as their first language. Sometimes they find keeping to the strict morals and traditions of Islam difficult, especially if they mix with non-Muslims at school and have non-Muslim friends. Islam affects their relationship with the opposite sex, family life, their recreation, the food they eat and the clothes they wear. Some rebel against their religious rules; many keep to the basic beliefs and principles of Islam; others are drawn to extreme anti-western Islamic organizations.

What does Islam say about drugs?

Islam permits the use of medicinal drugs, but drug use for recreation is forbidden, for the same reason as alcohol. Drugs can affect people's judgement and damage their health. There are social reasons too. Drug addicts can find it hard to hold down a job, and some commit crimes to feed their habit. Smoking tobacco is not forbidden to Muslims, perhaps because the dangers of nicotine were not recognized when these rules were made.

What does Islam say about gambling?

Islam forbids gambling in any form, so it was a great embarrassment to the Muslim community in England when one of the first winners of the national lottery turned out to be a Muslim! He was advised that it would be wrong of him to use the money for himself or his family, but that he could give it to charity. Islam teaches that people should earn money for themselves and their family through honest work.

All forms of gambling, including cards, roulette, horse racing, the pools and lottery, are forbidden to Muslims.

Do Muslims believe in the sanctity of life?

Islam teaches that all life is sacred because it is given by God, the Creator. This belief is at the heart of all Muslim teaching on mercy-killing, suicide, abortion, contraception, execution, war and murder.

Muslims believe that this life is supremely important because it is a person's chance to prepare for the life to come. The length of one's life on Earth should be left to God to decide and it is wrong for anyone to cut short a life except through due process of law. The Qur'an states: 'No-one dies unless Allah permits. The term of every life is fixed.'

From this Islamic principle, suicide and murder are clearly wrong. Nor is euthanasia permitted. This is sometimes called mercy-killing – helping people to die quickly and avoid more pain when their suffering is beyond medical help.

DEBATE - Are abortions acceptable?

- Yes: A woman's body is her own, and the foetus is part of her body until it can live separately from her. A woman has the right to put her own health and well-being before that of her foetus. Every child should be a wanted child. People also argue that a child that will be born severely handicapped should be aborted.

- No. Modern medicine can keep alive babies born after only five months of pregnancy. What right has anyone to destroy such a life? If God has allowed a life to come into being, it is arrogance for humans to think that they can override that.

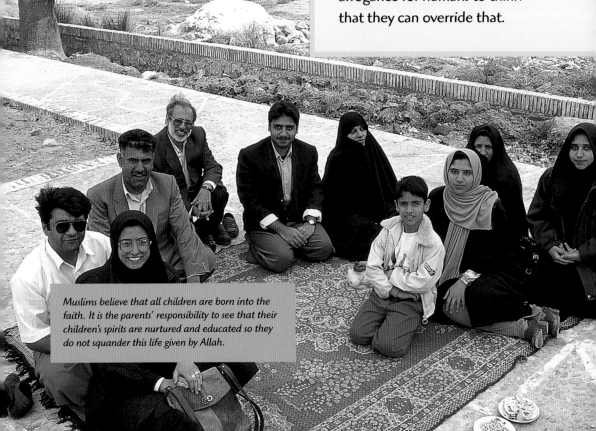

Muslims believe that all children are born into the faith. It is the parents' responsibility to see that their children's spirits are nurtured and educated so they do not squander this life given by Allah.

Muslim customs allow women to use contraceptive pills, which are taken every day, as these prevent the release of eggs produced within a woman's body.

Abortion – terminating a pregnancy – is also forbidden, unless the mother's life is at risk. A pregnancy can terminate naturally, but it can also be brought on medically. Modern technology can produce photographs of a foetus developing in the womb, so one can no longer think of a foetus as a 'blob of jelly' that becomes a person only at birth. Islam teaches that the soul enters the foetus at 120 days (four months) after conception, and if a miscarriage takes place after this time, or the baby is stillborn, then it would be buried in the same way as any other Muslim.

Is contraception allowed?

Birth control is allowed in Islam if it prevents conception taking place. Therefore, using a condom is permitted but using the morning-after pill is not because the child may already have been conceived, and this would cause an abortion.

Natural methods of contraception, such as withdrawal, were practised in Muhammad's time, and he permitted it. Muslims believe that creation ultimately lies in Allah's hands, so they should not prevent a birth if He wills it.

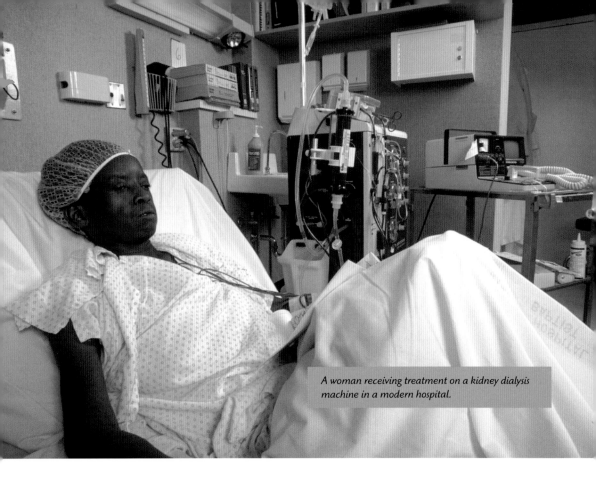

A woman receiving treatment on a kidney dialysis machine in a modern hospital.

Does modern medicine affect Muslims?

Modern medical techniques, such as embryo technology, organ transplants and the separation of conjoined twins, have raised issues for Islam that are obviously not dealt with directly in the Qur'an. In such cases, the basic Qur'anic principles have to be applied to the new situations.

For instance, artificial insemination by the husband, or *in vitro* fertilization of the wife's egg by the husband's sperm, is usually acceptable because these methods are helping the normal process for that couple to have their baby. But artificial insemination by a donor, and not the husband, is not acceptable because this is seen as similar to the sin of adultery, or having sex with someone other than one's husband or wife.

Doctors can now often separate twins that are joined at birth. This may mean that one of the twins will die, for instance if they share a heart. Then, the operation would only be performed if both twins were likely to die without it. Even so, it is difficult for Muslim parents to give consent to such an operation, knowing that saving the life of one of their children will hasten the death of another. The decision may be taken out of the parents' hands, and the babies are made wards of court, so that a judge decides on the best course of action.

Muslims have generally been opposed to organ transplants because of their belief in the resurrection, or rising up, of the body after death, at the Last Day. This is also the reason why they bury their dead, rather than cremate them.

They think it wrong to tamper with the body that God has created. However, this has caused problems for Muslims suffering from liver disease, which is particularly high in the Asian population, and some Muslim organizations now permit Muslims to donate and receive organs.

What about the sanctity of animal life?

The life of an animal is also sacred to Muslims. However, Muslims believe it is permissible to kill animals for food, but never to waste an animal's life. Muhammad lived in Arabia, a region with large expanses of desert. People kept herds of goats and sheep for food, because it was so dificult to grow food by farming the dry land. Without more water, crops such as vegetables could not be grown. The main agricultural crop came from date palms, which grow in desert oases.

There are strict food laws in Islam (just as there are in Judaism). Food that is 'permitted' is called halal and that which is not permitted is called haram. All fish, fruits and vegetables, and all grains, are permitted. Meat is permitted as long as it is slaughtered correctly – except for the pig, which is regarded as a dirty animal that causes disease. The halal method of slaughter is to slit the animal's throat with a very sharp knife, so that the animal does not feel the cut and quickly loses consciousness as the blood pours out. This is believed to be the most merciful method of killing. The name of God is pronounced over the animal in a prayer to remind Muslims that they are taking a life that comes from God – for all life is sacred.

Eating meat

Religions have different beliefs about meat-eating. Buddhists, for example, have compassion for all living things so they are usually vegetarians. Muslims, by contrast, are actually required to offer an animal sacrifice on the Great Pilgrimage. In the West, people tend to be protected from the issue of killing animals for food. It goes on out of sight, and meat usually comes ready packaged, or it is processed into prepared kinds of meat, such as sausages or burgers. Many Westerners, therefore, seldom need to confront openly that they kill animals for food.

All meat in Muslim countries is halal, that is, permitted for Muslims to eat. In non-Muslim countries, Muslims try to buy all their food from halal butcher shops, such as the one in Manchester, England, shown here.

If life is sacred, how can war be holy?

Muslims believe in the sanctity of life, and are therefore opposed to unlawful killing. However, the taking of life by lawful execution or when war has been declared, is considered to be justified.

Most people dislike the idea of war. However, in desperate situations, parents may feel proud of their children who are going off to war, while still worrying about their safety. In the same way, some religions have drawn up rules that make war permissible, a justified 'holy war'. In Islam, a war is considered to be holy if it is 'in the cause of Allah' – for justice and the right to practise Islam, and not for personal gain.

A holy war can only be undertaken as a last resort. It must have the authority of Muslim religious leaders and produce the minimum suffering necessary to win. Violence should stop when the enemy has surrendered; also, women, children, the elderly and disabled should not be harmed.

Are all Muslims militants?

In Islam, holy war is called jihad, which means 'striving'. Muhammad said the Greater Jihad is the struggle in each person to resist evil and the Lesser Jihad is taking up weapons to fight.

Muslims are taught that they should struggle against wrongdoing and oppression, and not just allow it to carry on. They should be prepared to give up everything, even their own lives, for the cause of right. In this sense, all Muslims should be militants – fighting against evil, but not in the sense of being aggressive or necessarily taking up weapons. Someone can struggle against evil in society, for example, through political channels. They can speak out against injustice and make their views heard.

Demonstrators in London's Trafalgar Square protest at the Israeli action against the Palestinians in the Middle East, where extremist Jews and Muslims clash constantly. Both sides of the dispute claim it is a just war.

Muslim clerics of the International Muslim Organization address a conference of Muslim leaders from communities in Great Britain. The meeting was held to discuss their views on 'jihad' – holy war – following the Muslim terrorist attack on the World Trade Center twin towers in New York on 11 September 2001.

When people hear of Muslims involved in conflicts around the world – the Palestinians and Jews; al-Qaida and the United States or its supporters; the Taliban conquerors of Afghanistan; the Indonesian extremists – the reports differ according to the perspective of the reporter. Are these Muslims freedom-fighters or terrorists? Are they suicide bombers or martyrs? Are their battles a Holy War, in fulfilment of the conditions for jihad, or have they little to do with their religion? Are they good Muslims or not? People must be careful not to judge any religion by everyone who claims they are believers in that faith.

DEBATE – Is violence ever justified?

- Yes. Violence is evil, but may be the lesser of two evils – for example, to overthrow a dictator whose actions are causing innocent people to suffer.

- No. The principle of 'an eye for an eye' will leave the whole world blind. If people are strong enough, they can overcome evil with love.

One meaning of 'Islam' is peace, and Muslims greet each other with the words *Salaam aleikum* – Peace be with you. Islam teaches that people shall find peace with themselves and with each other through submission to the will of God.

REFERENCE

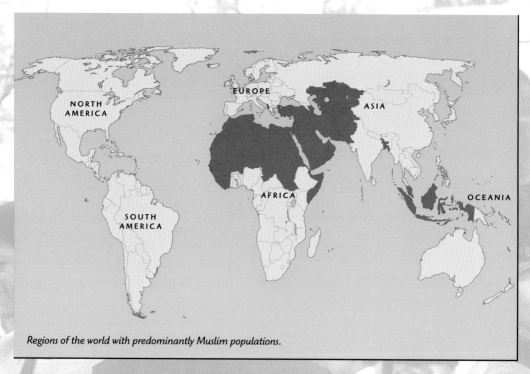

Regions of the world with predominantly Muslim populations.

Islam – worldwide distribution

There are up to 1 300 million Muslims in the world – one in five of the human population, and it is the fastest growing religion. Muslims live in all continents of the world. Although their numbers are relatively small in Europe, Islam is the second largest religion in the UK after Christianity.

Islam, as we know it, began in Arabia during the time of Muhammad, but quickly spread beyond Arabia (now Saudi Arabia), and only 20% of Muslims are now Arabs. Makkah, in Saudi Arabia, remains the religious centre of Islam.

Most Muslims still live in the countries to which Islam spread in its first century: Egypt, Libya, Tunisia and Algeria, which stretch along the north coast of Africa, and the countries of the Middle East such as Jordan, Iraq, Iran and Afghanistan.

Other countries where Muslims form over 90% of the population now include some West African countries, such as Mauritania and Mali, Asian countries such as Pakistan, countries of the Russian Federation such as Chechnya, and Indonesia in South-east Asia. The countries with the highest number of Muslims are Indonesia with 160 million and Pakistan with 130 million. Both are densely populated.

Language

Arabic is the language of the Muslim holy book, the Qur'an, because Muhammad lived in Arabia (now Saudi Arabia). Arabic is also the dominant spoken language in the Muslim countries of Jordan, Iraq and Syria and also the countries of North Africa, down to Mauritania in western Africa and including the Sudan, which is south of Egypt.

Timeline of Islam

CE (Common Era)

570	Birth of Muhammad.
610	First revelation of the Qur'an to Muhammad.
622	The Hijrah: Emigration of Muhammad to Madinah. (This date marks the beginning of the Muslim calendar).
630	Muhammad conquered Makkah and made it the centre of Islam.
632	Muhammad died.
661	The political centre of Islam moved to Damascus in Syria.
750	The political centre of Islam moved to Baghdad in Iraq. This remained the centre for the next 500 years.
900–1200	Islamic science and arts flourished.
1500–1700	Islamic empires at their height, e.g. the Mughals in India.
1924	The last Islamic empire, the Ottoman Caliphate, was disbanded after 400 years.
1947	The new Muslim country of Pakistan was created.
1971	Bangladesh, a new Muslim country, broke away from Pakistan.
1977–1979	A revolution in Iran re-established Islamic law.

Festivals

Name	Western calendar	Muslim month
Muharram	May/June	Muharram
Festival of Ashura	May/June	Muharram
Ramadan starts	January/February	Ramadan
Lailat-ul-Qadr	January	Ramadan
Id-ul-Fitr	February	Ramadan
8–13 Dhu-l-Hija	April/May	Dhu-l-Hija
Id-ul-Adha	April/May	Dhu-l-Hija
Maulid Al Nabi	July/August	Rabi' I

The Six Major Faiths

BUDDHISM
Founded
535 BCE in Northern India

Number of followers
Estimated at 360 million

Holy Places
Bodh Gaya, Sarnath, both in northern India

Holy Books
Tripitaka

Holy Symbol
Eight-spoked wheel

JUDAISM
Founded
In what is now Israel, around 2000 BCE

Number of followers
Around 13 million religious Jews

Holy Places
Jerusalem, especially the Western Wall

Holy Books
The Torah

Holy Symbol
Seven-branched menorah (candle stand)

CHRISTIANITY
Founded
Around 30 CE, Jerusalem

Number of followers
Just under 2 000 million

Holy Places
Jerusalem and other sites associated with the life of Jesus

Holy Books
The Bible (Old and New Testament)

Holy Symbol
Cross

HINDUISM
Founded
Developed gradually in prehistoric times

Number of followers
Around 750 million

Holy Places
River Ganges, especially at Varanasi (Benares). Several other places in India

Holy Books
Vedas, Upanishads, Mahabharata, Ramayana

Holy Symbol
Aum

SIKHISM
Founded Northwest India, 15th century CE

Number of followers 22.8 million

Holy Places
There are five important, takhts, or seats of high authority: in Amritsar, Patna Sahib, Anandpur Sahib, Nanded and Talwandi.

Sacred Scripture
The Guru Granth Sahib

Holy Symbol
The Khanda, the symbol of the Khalsa.

ISLAM
Founded
610 CE in Arabia (modern Saudi Arabia).

Number of followers
Over 1 000 million

Holy Places
Makkah and Madinah, in Saudi Arabia

Holy Books
The Qur'an

Holy Symbol
Crescent and star

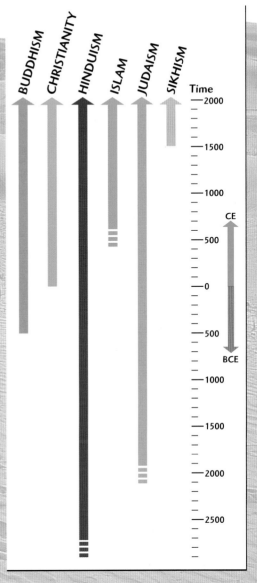

While some faiths can point to a definite time and person for their origin, others can not. For example, Muslims teach that the beliefs of Islam predate Muhammad and go back to the beginning of the world. Hinduism apparently developed from several different prehistoric religious traditions.

GLOSSARY

Al-Amin 'The Trustworthy', name by which the Prophet Muhammad was generally known, even before the revelation of Islam.

Allah Arabic name used for God in Islam in preference to the word for 'God'; has no plural and no gender-distinctive characteristics.

Allahu Akbar The words in Arabic for 'Allah is most great.'

Bismillah The words in Arabic for 'In the name of Allah'.

Bismillah-ir-Rahman-ir-Rahim 'In the name of Allah – All Gracious, All Merciful', said by Muslims before eating or performing some action.

Dhu-l-Hijah Month of the Hajj, last month of the Islamic year.

Hadith Saying, report, account – the sayings of the Prophet Muhammad, as recounted by his household, descendants and companions.

Hafiz Someone who knows the whole Qur'an by heart.

Hajj Annual pilgrimage to Makkah, which each Muslim must undertake at least once in a lifetime if he or she is fit enough and can afford to do so.

halal Anything that is permitted or lawful in Islam.

haram Anything unlawful or not permitted in Islam.

hijab 'Veil', most often used to describe the headscarf or modest dress Muslims believe should be worn by women.

Hijrah Departure, exit, emigration – the emigration of the Prophet Muhammad from Makkah to Madinah in 622 CE; the event that starts the Islamic calendar.

Id Recurring happiness – religious holiday; a feast for thanking Allah and celebrating a happy occasion. Id-ul-Adha and Id-ul-Fitr are major holidays.

Id Mubarak 'Id blessings!'– greeting exchanged during Islamic celebrations.

Id-ul-Adha Celebration of the sacrifice, commemorating the Prophet Ibrahim's willingness to sacrifice his son Isma'il for Allah.

Id-ul-Fitr Celebration of breaking the fast on the day after Ramadan ends; the first day of Shawal, the tenth Islamic month.

ihram State or condition entered into to perform Hajj; also, the name given to the two plain white unsewn clothes worn by male pilgrims, or to the modest clothing worn by women pilgrims.

imam 'Leader', someone who leads the communal prayer, or a founder of an Islamic school of jurisprudence; also, in Shi'ah Islam, the title of Ali and his successors.

Islam Peace attained through willing obedience to Allah's divine guidance; the religion based on this principle.

Jibreel Gabriel, the angel who delivered Allah's messages to his Prophets.

jihad Personal, individual struggle against evil in the way of Allah; also, defence of the Muslim community, a 'holy war'.

jumu'ah Weekly communal salah (prayer), and attendance at the khutbah (speech) performed shortly after midday on Fridays.

Ka'bah Cube-shaped structure in the centre of the grand mosque in Makkah; the first house built for the worship of the One True God.

khutbah 'Speech', talk delivered on special occasions, such as the jumu'ah, and Id prayers.

Lailat-ul-Qadr The Night of Power, when the first revelation of the Qur'an was made to the Prophet Muhammad.

masjid Place of prostration, mosque.

minbar A small set of steps in a mosque from which a sermon is given.

mu'adhin Call to prayer; known in English as 'muezzin'.

Muharram First month in the Islamic calendar, calculated precisely from the time that the Prophet Muhammad migrated to Madinah.

Muslim One who claims to have accepted Islam by professing the Shahadah (declaration of faith).

prophet A man or woman who acts as a messenger from God.

Qur'an The holy book of Islam, believed to contain Allah's actual words, as revealed to Muhammad.

Ramadan Ninth month of the Islamic calendar, when fasting is required from just before dawn until sunset, as ordered by Allah in the Qur'an.

revelation Knowledge that is revealed to a person by God.

salah Five different prayers, recited every day in Arabic, in the manner taught by the Prophet Muhammad, spread at intervals from first thing in the morning until last thing at night.

Sawm Fasting from just before dawn until sunset; abstinence from all food and drink (including water) as well as smoking and sex.

Shahadah Declaration of faith, consisting of the statement: 'There is no god except Allah. Muhammad is the Messenger of Allah.'

Shari'ah Islamic law based on the Qur'an and the Sunnah (a collection of model practices).

Shi'a 'Followers', that is, Muslims who believe in the Imamah: the successorship of Ali, after the Prophet Muhammad, and 11 of his most pious and most knowledgeable descendants.

Sunnah Model practices, customs and traditions of the Prophet Muhammad.

Sunni Muslims who believe in the successorship of Abu Bakr, Umar, Uthman and Ali, after the Prophet Muhammad.

wudu Ablution performed before salah (ritual prayer).

Zakah Purification of wealth by payment of an annual welfare due – an obligatory act of worship.

FURTHER INFORMATION

BOOKS and MAGAZINES

School textbooks with information covering the main aspects of Islam.

Less detailed:
Islam, Andrew Egan, Heinemann 2002

The Muslim Experience, Aylett & O'Donnell, Hodder & Stoughton 2000

Islam for Today, Angela Wood, Oxford University Press 1998

More detailed:
Islam, Janet Green, Hodder & Stoughton 2001

Islam in today's world, Clinton, Lynch, Orchard, Weston & Wright, John Murray 1999

Islam. A new approach, Jan Thompson, Hodder & Stoughton 1998

An easy book for the general reader:
Teach Yourself Islam, Ruqaiyyah Maqsood, Hodder & Stoughton 1994 (New series May 2003)

ORGANIZATIONS

IQRA Trust
A leading British Muslim educational charity engaged in education and information on Islam. It works with LEAs, schools and teachers in many ways to provide information about Islam. It has an enquiry service, a wide range of publications and an Interactive Islamic Experience Exhibition.
IQRA Trust, 24 Culross Street, London W1Y 3HE, UK
0207 491 1572
Website: www.info@iqratrust.org

The Islamic Foundation
UK-based institution for education, research, publications and training on Islam; works with inter-faith groups.
The Islamic Foundation, 223 London Road, Leicester LE2 1ZE, UK
Website: www.islamic-foundation.org.uk

WEBSITES

www.mcb.org.uk/member.html
Membership list of The Muslim Council
of Britain, listing many useful Islamic
organizations.

www.soundvision.com
USA website for Islamic information
and products.

info@muslimnews.co.uk
News items about Muslims and the
Islamic world.

www.islamic-centre.org.uk
www.islamicculturalcentre.co.uk
Websites for the London Central
Mosque Trust and The Islamic Cultural
Centre (housed at this mosque), which
include an introduction to Islam, history
of the mosque, prayer-times and more.

www.muslimaid.org
International relief and development
agency working to alleviate poverty and
suffering among some of the world's
poorest people.

**www.beliefnet.com (use a search
engine for Hajj)**
Information and personal accounts of
Hajj.

INDEX